David, the Shepherd Boy.

A Cantata in Ten Scenes,

for

The Choir and the Choral Society,

with numbers for children's voices, if desired.

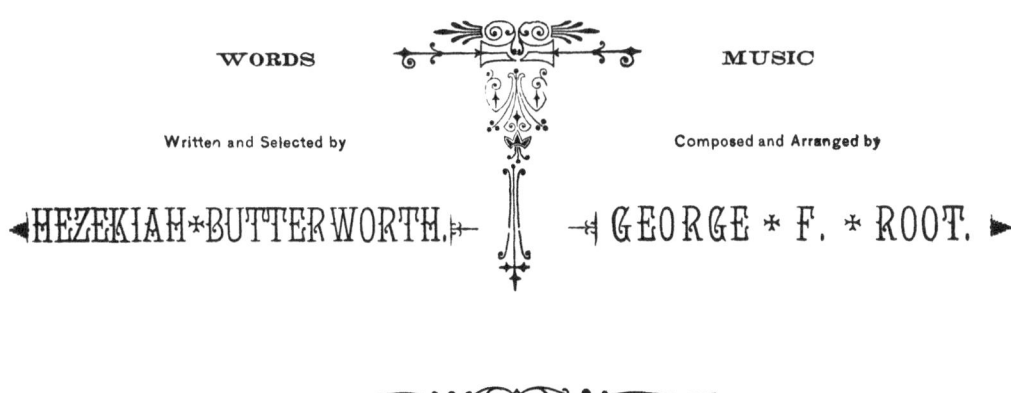

WORDS
Written and Selected by
Hezekiah Butterworth.

MUSIC
Composed and Arranged by
George F. Root.

Fredonia Books
Amsterdam, The Netherlands

David, The Shepherd Boy:
A Cantata in Ten Scenes for the Choir and the
Choral Society

Words Written and Selected by
Hezekiah Butterworth

Music Composed and Arranged by
George F. Root

ISBN: 1-4101-0264-5

Copyright © 2003 by Fredonia Books

Fredonia Books
Amsterdam, The Netherlands
http://www.fredoniabooks.com

All rights reserved, including the right to reproduce
this book, or portions thereof, in any form.

In order to make original editions of historical works
available to scholars at an economical price, this
facsimile of the original edition is reproduced from
the best available copy and has been digitally
enhanced to improve legibility, but the text remains
unaltered to retain historical authenticity.

CONTENTS.

	Page
SCENE FIRST. THE FEAST OF TRUMPETS AT BETHLEHEM	5
SCENE SECOND. ABIGAIL AT CARMEL	26
SCENE THIRD. SAUL IN DESPONDENCY	32
SCENE FOURTH. DIALOGUE. TWO SENTINELS	38
SCENE FIFTH. AFTER THE BATTLE	39
SCENE SIXTH. DAVID IN EXILE	51
SCENE SEVENTH. DAVID AND THE SHEPHERD QUEEN	57
SCENE EIGHTH. THE CARMELITE BRIDE	66
SCENE NINTH. THE EVENING BEFORE THE CORONATION	73
SCENE TENTH. THE CORONATION	79
For the Joyous Feast. Chorus	5
The Coming of Samuel. Solo and Chorus	9
Ye Sons of Boaz and of Ruth	10
Let Us Rejoice. Chorus	11
The Anointing. Recitative and Chorus	16
Interlude. The Coming of David	20
I am David the Shepherd Boy. Song	21
Tableau and Chorus. The Lord is High and Holy	23
Sing, Children of Bethlehem, Sing. Children's Chorus	24
How Happy are the Children. Obligato for Children and Chorus	25
O Carmel Fair! Song and Duet	26
A Shepherd There Was. Song and Quartet	28
Thou Singest of Judah. Recitative	29
O Abigail, Queen of Carmel! Recitative. O Crystal Night! Quartet	30
Sad is the Heart. Song	32
Fair Shepherd. Song	34
Harp Interlude	35
Forsaken! Song	36
A Thousand Men. Chorus of Women	39
Recitatives. O King! I Have Sought for Thee the Lad, etc.	40
Now Take the Tabrets. Chorus	42
O Shepherd! Song	45
O Lord, Our Lord! Song	46
When Heroes Return. Chorus	47
In Awful Caverns. Song	51
But That, Alas! Trio	52
We Have Broken Our Way. Recitative	53
Oh, Why is Thy Soul! Trio	54
As Pants the Hart. Song and accompanying Trio	55
Nabal doth Scorn My Suit. Recitative	57
The Shepherds Shear Their Fleecy Flocks. Song and Chorus	58
Blessed be the Lord. Recitative	62
O David, Thy Foe hath Perished! Recitative	64
The Rosy Heights of Carmel. Chorus of Children	65
From Carmel We Come. Bridal March and Chorus	66
Oh, Long Hast Thou Wandered! Song and Refrain	71
The Lord My Shepherd Is. Harp Song	73
Hail! and Manasseh Sends Her Thousands. Double Chorus	79
Interlude during the crowning	82
As Mountains 'round His People Rise. Quartet and Obligato Solo	83
Hosanna! Blessed is He that Cometh. Finale	85

DIRECTIONS.

"DAVID, THE SHEPHERD BOY," may be given as a concert, book in hand, without curtain or costumes, or it may be given with the accessories of appropriate decorations, costumes, and action.

Where the latter plan is adopted the following remarks and suggestions will be found useful:

This Cantata is in Ten Scenes, but not in Ten Parts. The frequent use of the curtain is not for rest or intermission, but to allow the singers to make necessary changes without anxiety or appearance of confusion. This plan will also help the audience to imagine the change of location that takes place with nearly every scene.

The curtain should remain down but a minute, or two minutes at most, so that the interest may be kept up after it is once aroused.

It will be an excellent plan, in giving this Cantata, to have a good full chorus of children. They might be seated in front of platform and curtain, where they could sing their pieces and join in the others as marked. They need not take part in the action, though by sitting somewhat sidewise to the audience they could look upon the platform and so participate in, and enjoy the parts assigned to the older ones.

This plan in regard to the children is proposed because the platform can not have seats upon it (where the piece is given with costumes and action), and the children should be seated when they are not singing, and because considerable free room will be required for the best effect of some of the scenes.

The Cantata can be given without the children's voices, by omitting the numbers marked especially for them.

It will be seen that some of the numbers are for children alone, some are for more mature voices alone, and some for both together. Those that are for the children alone are marked "Children," those that are for the adults alone are marked "Choir," and those that are for both together are marked "Full Chorus."

The solo parts have been prepared with reference to the more mature voices, as follows:

ABIGAIL	Soprano.
ABIGAIL's two Attendants	Soprano and Alto.
MICHAL	Alto.
DAVID	Tenor.
JESSE	Baritone.
SAMUEL	Base.
SAUL	Base.
ELDER (who crowns David)	Base.
ABNER and Messenger	Baritone or Tenor

Three men of war. Quartets of Shepherds. Two Sentinels.

All of the scenes presumably take place out of doors, so that boughs of trees, festoons of evergreens, and floral decorations about the platform would be appropriate.

Beyond this, a side tent for the Third Scene and something to answer for a throne in the last scene, would be desirable. It would be well to have the throne on a little elevation (perhaps six or eight inches above the platform), and large enough to hold the five who take part in the last quartet and obligato. The throne may be a large chair with such decorations as may be convenient, and perhaps a canopy. The tent is put up for the Third Scene only and then withdrawn. As only the end of a tent projecting a little from one side is needed, it may be imitated with white paper or muslin, and so be light, and easily put on and withdrawn.

There may be a bed of grasses and flowers in Scene Sixth, over which David can pour the water which the three men bring him, but that is not essential. David may appear to pour the water without doing so, or he may set the goblet aside.

Tabrets or timbrels were like tambourines, and were worn on cords around the neck. They may be easily imitated by round boxes or their covers.

David's costume at first is a tunic with girdle, and a scrip or wallet hung over his shoulder and falling by his side. He also bears a staff with a shepherd's crook at the end. Head dress something like a turban. In exile David has tunic, girdle and spear. The same on meeting Abigail (some light color not bright or conspicuous.) At coronation a flowing robe of bright cambric in imitation of royal robes. The girdle may be jewelled or otherwise ornamented. Scepter and crown—the first covered with gilt paper, the second made of pasteboard and gilt paper.

Samuel appears as an aged patriarch with long white beard; in flowing robes of black cambric, and girdled, or with a girdle tied loosely and falling to the floor. Turban. He will have in his hand a "horn of oil," or some ornamental vessel supposed to contain oil. As Samuel does not appear after the First Scene, the person who takes that part may assume one of the others that follow, provided his appearance can be sufficiently changed.

Saul appears with a crown. It may, perhaps, be the same that is placed upon David's head in the last scene. His costume may consist of a long robe of cambric embroidered with gold thread or any tasteful ornament.

Jesse has simply a shepherd's costume.

The "men of war" may be represented with helmets, breastplates and spears; otherwise as shepherds.

Helmets and breastplates are imitated by pasteboard covered with tin-foil or enamelled paper. Shepherds are transformed into soldiers or warriors by the addition of breastplates and spears. Shepherds' costumes same as David's at first—frock or tunic, and girdle and crook.

If the children are in costume, simple sacques or tunics with girdles would be proper; the girls' dresses brighter and more tastefully prepared.

This Cantata will be just the right length for an evening's entertainment if there are no delays between the scenes. If, however, it is found best to shorten it, omissions may be made of those numbers that can best be spared.

Female costumes will readily suggest themselves to those interested. They may be simple and of inexpensive material.

It will be remembered that bright cambric under artificial light has the effect of silk to an audience, and oriental impressions may be made by it as easily as by costly fabrics.

The coming of Abigail as a bride should be made the occasion of as beautiful a floral display as possible, and she may be as richly dressed as is convenient.

DAVID, THE SHEPHERD BOY.

— SCENE FIRST. —

THE FEAST OF TRUMPETS AT BETHLEHEM.

No. 1. CHORUS. For the Joyous Feast.

SHEPHERDS & BETHLEHEMITES. All the singers take part at the commencement, excepting SAMUEL, DAVID, ABIGAIL and attendants, MICHAL & SAUL. The singers move about during the prelude, getting to their positions in time to commence the chorus. Keep well to the front, leaving space in center for the single voices.

*Throughout this work we shall, in modulations, allow one signature simply to displace another, and so avoid the use of unnecessary characters. Singers and players may imagine the naturals in such cases if they need them.

plenty dwells, Let sil-ver trumpets blow! With trumpet and horn Salute the morn, Let the silver trumpets blow, Let the sil-ver trumpets blow!

No. 2. The Coming of Samuel.

While the singers are looking toward the entrance at which SAMUEL is to appear, (making occasional and appropriate gestures) they should be careful to keep well turned toward the audience.

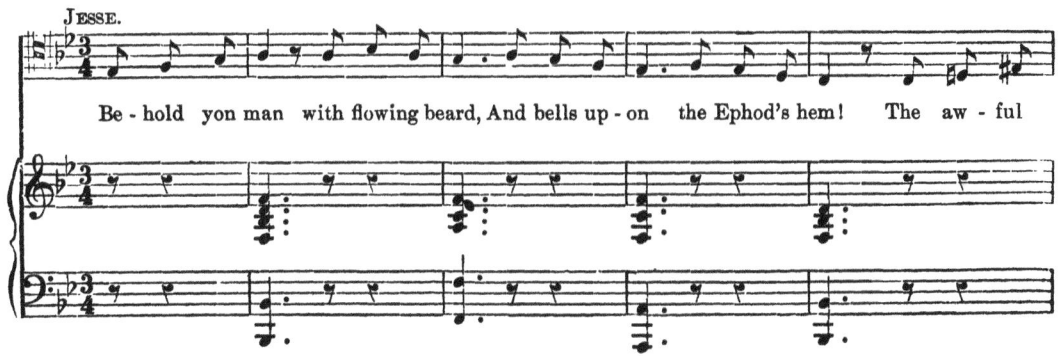

JESSE.
Be-hold yon man with flowing beard, And bells up-on the Ephod's hem! The aw-ful

11

No. 3. CHORUS. Let us rejoice.

12

Children may sing the Soprano of this movement, the Choir taking the other parts softly.

God is high and ho - ly, Yet lov-eth He the low - ly; The hum-ble He ex-

God is high and ho - ly, Yet lov-eth He the low - ly; The hum-ble He ex-

alt - eth, In Him we will re - joice; The hum-ble He ex - alt - eth, In

alt - eth, In Him we will re - joice; The hum-ble He ex - alt - eth, In

14

16

No. 4. The Anointing.

17

come to thee this day by God ap-point-ed, And from thy sons must choose the Lord's An-ointed. In Saul's proud heart no more is God re-spect-ed, And God his crown and scep-ter hath re-ject-ed. Let now thy sons ap-pear!

JESSE.
(To servant.) *(One of the Chorus steps forward.)* *(To Samuel.)*
Call thou E-li-ab. Be-hold him tall and fair!

18

SAMUEL.
During the interlude Samuel remains with bowed head and clasped hands, as if receiving from heaven the words that he announces.

The Lord refuseth this thy sec-ond son. Let yet the next ap-pear.

JESSE. (*Another steps forward.*)
I bring to thee my third son. He surely is the chosen one of Is-ra-el.

SAMUEL (*bowed as before.*)
Neither hath the Lord chosen this.

JESSE.
I bring to thee yet (*They step forward.*) seven sons. Among them must the Lord's Anointed be.

SAMUEL.
The Lord hath not chosen

20

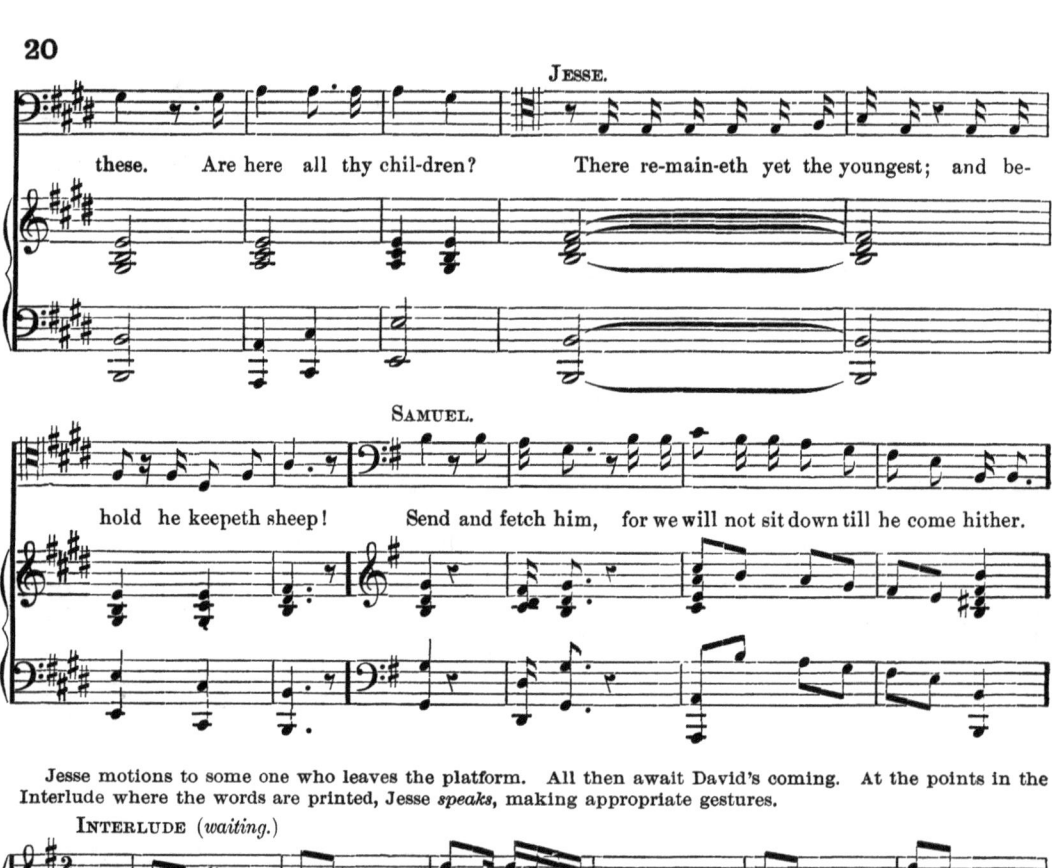

these.   Are here all thy chil-dren?   There re-main-eth yet the youngest; and be-hold he keepeth sheep!   Send and fetch him,   for we will not sit down till he come hither.

Jesse motions to some one who leaves the platform. All then await David's coming. At the points in the Interlude where the words are printed, Jesse *speaks*, making appropriate gestures.

Yonder he comes:

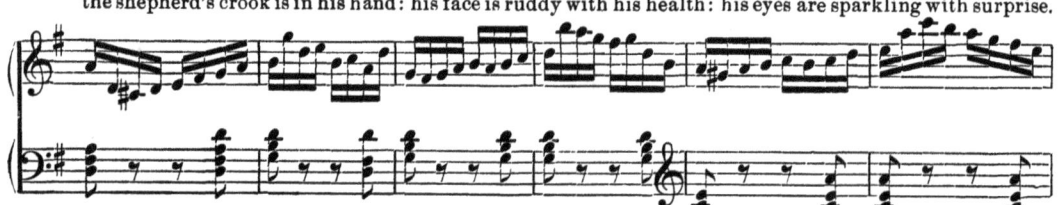

the shepherd's crook is in his hand: his face is ruddy with his health: his eyes are sparkling with surprise.

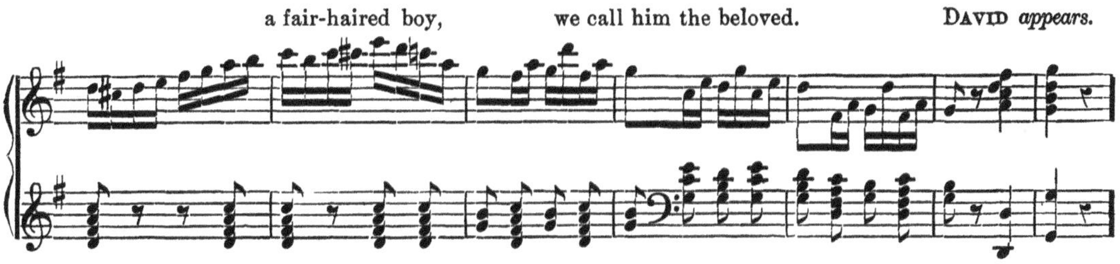

No. 5. SONG. I am David the Shepherd Boy.

22

Do not sing 2d verse, unless there is a demand for repetition. It is printed to be sung when the song is used separately from the Cantata.

23

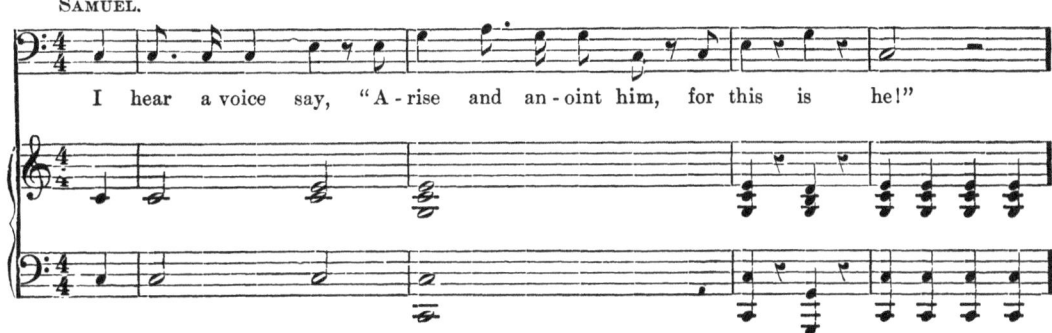

No. 6. TABLEAU.

David kneels at the feet of the Prophet, leaning on his crook. The Prophet holds over his head the horn of holy oil, as if preparing to pour it. All others on the platform assume appropriate positions of interest. Meanwhile, a few voices out of sight sing as follows, (without accompaniment if possible). The tableau should remain immoveable until a curtain conceals it, at or near the close of the singing.

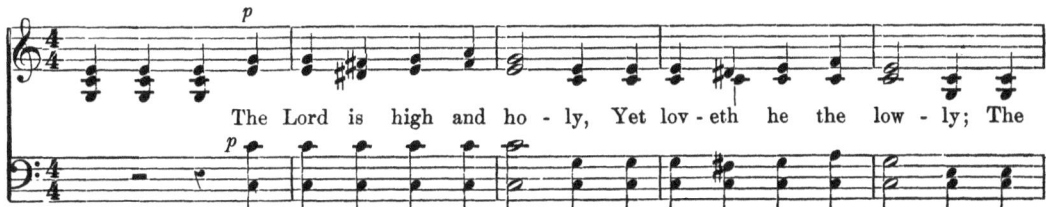

The voices should be kept subdued, though with a clear, joyful quality.

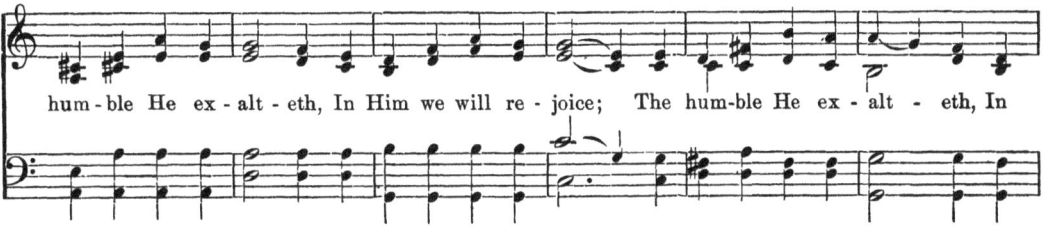

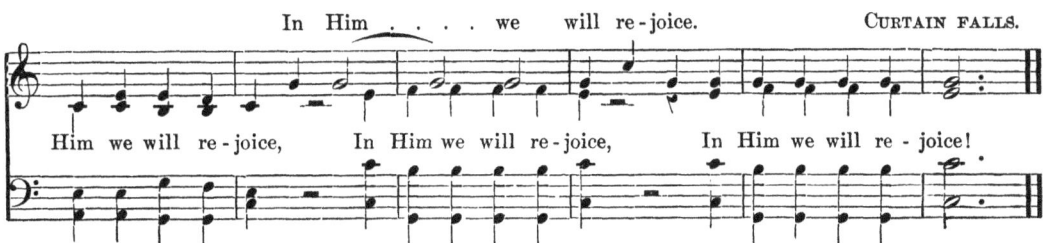

It should be remembered, all through, that the fall of the curtain does not indicate an intermission. It is simply to allow the singers to change their positions or retire, without awkwardness, and also to aid the audience to imagine the next scene in another place. The curtain should not be down more than a minute, or two minutes at the most.

No. 7. Sing, Children of Bethlehem.

If the children are in front of the curtain, this number may be sung while the curtain is down. If the children are on the platform, the curtain must be raised as soon as the Choir have had time to regain then position (or retire) after the Tableau.

CHILDREN.

1. Sing, chil-dren of Beth-le-hem, sing, The sor-row is turned in-to joy; From fold-ed flocks 'neath shel-ter-ing rocks, God call-eth His shep-herd boy.
2. He lov-eth the low-ly in heart, And near to the shep-herd boy drew, As 'neath the rocks, while slumbered the flocks, He prayed a-mid flowers and dew.

Bless-ed, oh, bless-ed are they who ear-ly heed Him! bless-ed the chil-dren who ear-ly seek His face. The lambs of His love and His care, the lit-tle ones, ev-er are near Him. Oh, may they not stray from wis-dom's way, but walk in her paths of peace!

No. 8. How Happy are the Children.

Let the Children sing their obligato *first alone*—the Choir part being used as an instrumental accompaniment—then Children and Adults, as marked. If the curtain has been raised for this number, it should fall for a minute or two, as the next Scene is supposed to be in another place.

26

—SCENE SECOND.—

ABIGAIL AT CARMEL.

No. 1. SONG. O Carmel Fair!

ABIGAIL with her two Attendants (Soprano and Alto.) SHEPHERDS (four or eight) with bunches of flowers in their crooks. For this scene, if convenient, the lights may be put down a little, that twilight may be represented.

O Carmel fair! whose peaks a-rise O'er Es-drælon's thrice-fruited trees; Bathed in the blue light of the skies, And laved for-ev-er by the seas, I love the green-ness

28

No. 2. SONG AND QUARTET. A Shepherd there was.
(Men's voices.)

29

pas-tor-al reeds play low, play sweet..) He touched the harp with a mys-tic hand, And the
pas-tor-al reeds play loud, play clear..) And oft in his rapt and mel-o-dious lays, He
pas-tor-al reeds play sweet, play clear..) Who charmed the flocks, and whose mystic strains The

white flocks lay.. at his feet, The white flocks lay.. at his feet.
felt his God... was near, He felt his God... was near.
Deities bowed.. to hear, The Dei-ties bowed.. to hear.

No. 3. Thou singest of Judah.

ABIGAIL. *Recitative.*

Thou sing-est of Ju-dah, Sing now of our own fair fields and downs; Be-hold Car-mel! how

30

No. 4. Recitative and Quartet of Men's Voices, and accompanying Trio of Women's Voices.

Take pains to speak exactly in unison and together, without instrument if possible.

RECITATIVE. O ABIGAIL, QUEEN OF CARMEL! ALL THE SHEPHERDS.

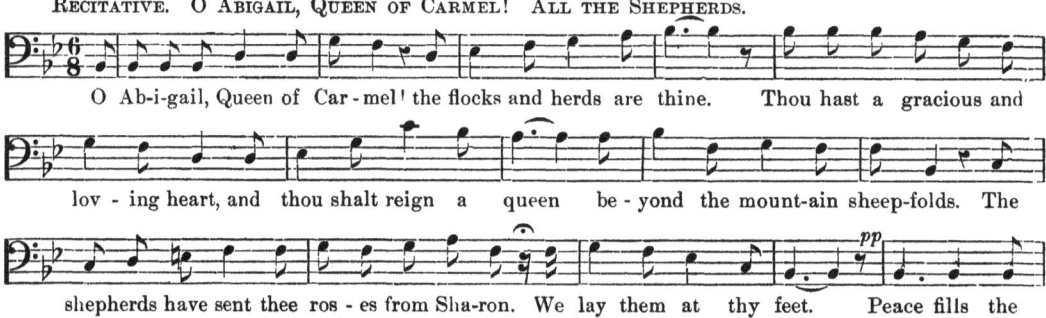

Carry the voices with a light thread of tone from "still" to "Crystal" without taking breath between those words. Take breath at the rest before "and still," and do not take breath again until after "night." Keep all *very soft* in the transition from the unison to the harmony.

QUARTET. O CRYSTAL NIGHT!

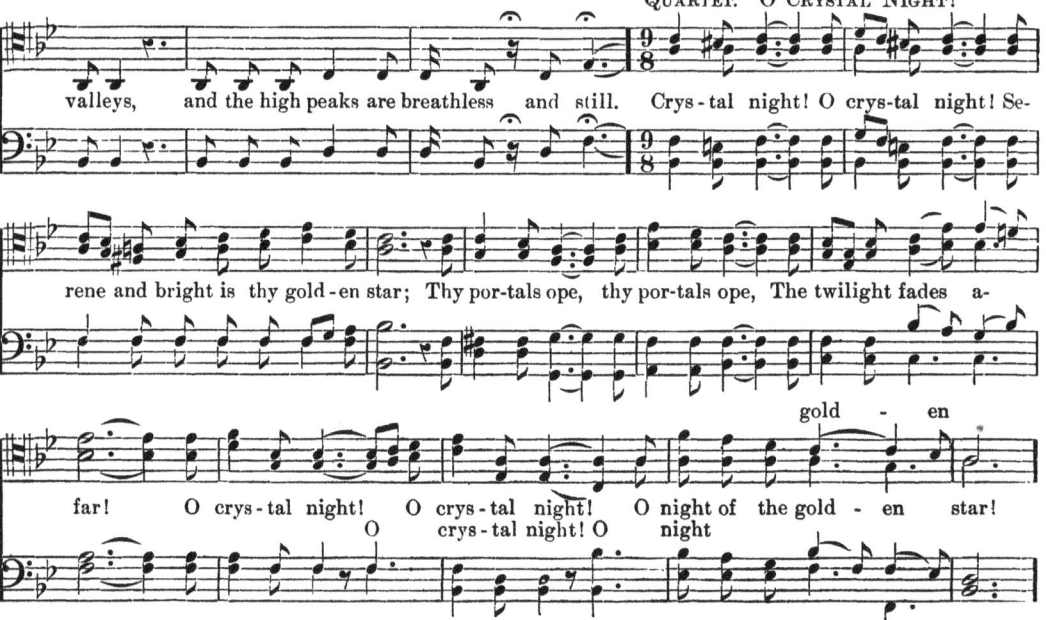

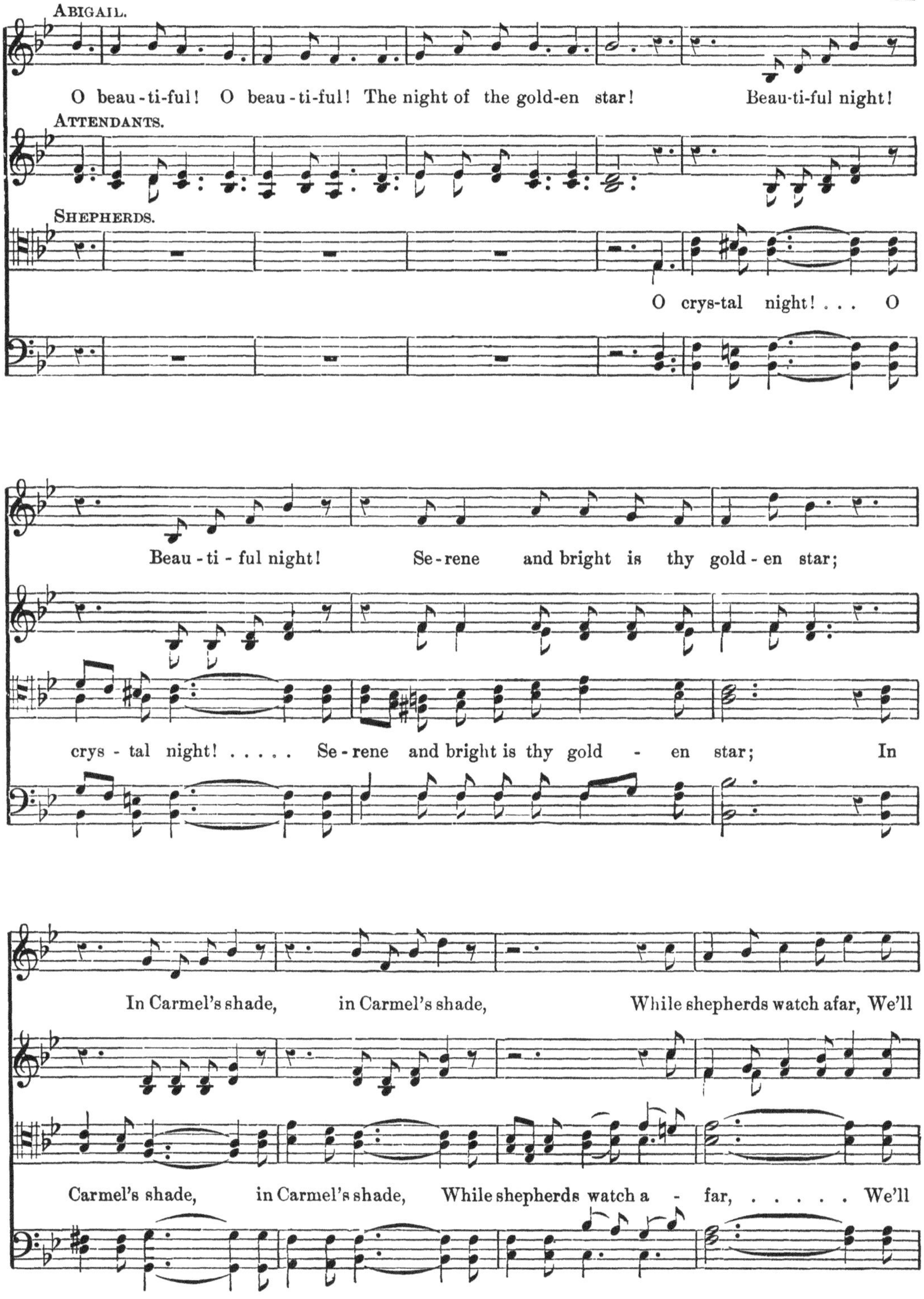
ABIGAIL.
O beau-ti-ful! O beau-ti-ful! The night of the gold-en star! Beau-ti-ful night!
ATTENDANTS.
SHEPHERDS.
O crys-tal night! . . . O
Beau-ti-ful night! Se-rene and bright is thy gold-en star;
crys-tal night! . . . . . Se-rene and bright is thy gold - en star; In
In Carmel's shade, in Carmel's shade, While shepherds watch afar, We'll
Carmel's shade, in Carmel's shade, While shepherds watch a - far, ... We'll

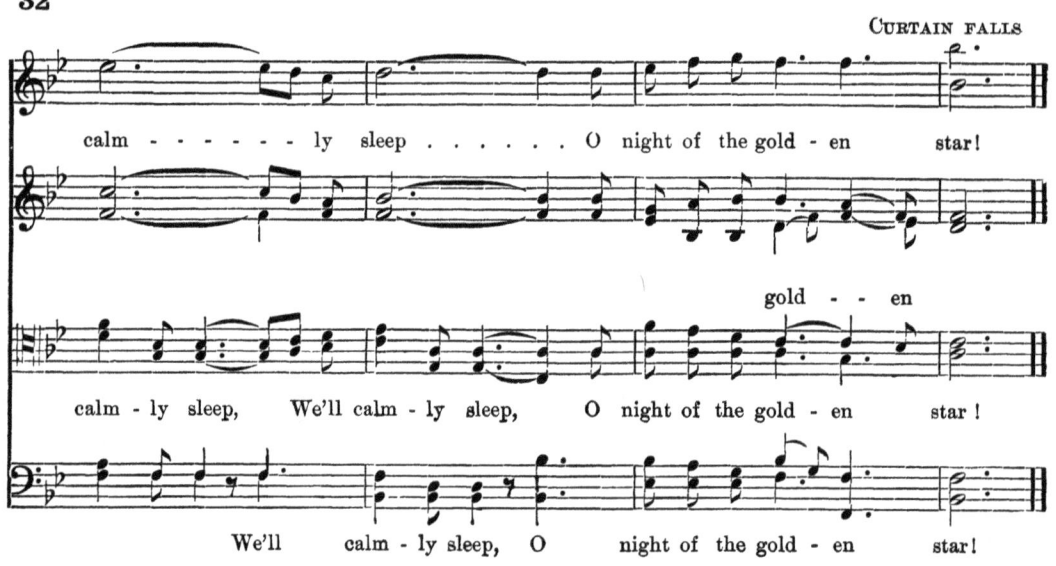

—SCENE THIRD.—

SAUL IN DESPONDENCY.

David in shepherd's garb. Michal, daughter of Saul. (If convenient, the opening of a tent may be seen on one side of the stage. If it is not convenient to have a harp, or the imitation of a harp, for David to appear to play upon during the harp-music on the piano, the harp-music may come from the side of the stage, from the tent if it is there, David retiring at the time. Of course, the best thing would be the real harp and real harp-music, but that would rarely be possible.)

No. 1 SONG. Sad is the Heart.

heart whose prayers no more The ear of God will hear; That sees, where
less of gold-en light, And ro-ses less each eve; I've lost from

se-raphs sang be-fore, But mocking shapes ap-pear. The harvest's past, the
life the old-en light, And all my hopes de-ceive; The harvest's past, the

sum-mer's fled, The light of youth is gone; My manhood's prime to
sum-mer's fled, The light of youth is gone; A-round me clust-er

Play Prelude for Interlude.

age is wed, And oft-en-times I feel with dread, Death's win-ter steal-ing on!
shapes of dread, And dark o'er my dis-crown-ed head, Des-pair is steal-ing on!

No. 3. Harp Interlude.

Imitation of Harp. Saul grows more quiet during the interlude.

No. 4. SONG. Forsaken.

Harp Interlude. Concluded.

At the close of the Interlude Saul sleeps.

—SCENE FOURTH.—

DIALOGUE.

The speakers in this part will stand near the end of the stage opposite that of the tent scene. They will seem to be looking at a scene the audience can not see.

Two sentinels on the hills, looking down on the valley of the Terebinth, where the Jewish and Philistine armies are drawn up in order of battle.

1st. Sentinel.—How goeth the battle in the valley of Elah?

2d. Sentinel.—Look you yonder to the open space between the armies. Such a scene never was heard of in Judah before.

1st. Sentinel.—It is Goliath of Gath. We have fallen upon evil times, for Israel hath no champion that can meet him. His height is six cubits and a span. He hath a helmet of brass and a coat of mail, and the weight of his coat is five thousand shekels.

2d. Sentinel.—He hath just come forward, swelling with pride, and hath defied the armies of Israel. But, look again—what dost thou see?

1st. Sentinel.—A boy with a staff in his hand. He carries a sling, and at his side is a shepherd's bag. Saul hath offered great honors and riches, and hath promised his daughter in marriage to him who will prevail against this giant. He surely hath not confided his cause to a boy. But, the giant is proudly boasting—what doth he say?

2d. Sentinel.—He saith to the lad: "I will give thy flesh to the fowls of the air and the beasts of the field." [Pause.]

1st. Sentinel.—What doth the lad reply?

2d. Sentinel.—He answereth nobly, and saith: "I come to thee in the name of the Lord of hosts; the God of the armies of Israel, whom thou hast defied."

1st. Sentinel.—The mighty giant hath fallen! Israel is free! Who is this champion that hath done the mighty deed? He hath slain Goliath with a pebble from his sling. Surely, such a thing was never known in Israel.

2d. Sentinel.—The Philistines flee. Let us descend to the plain. [Curtain falls.]

39

SCENE FIFTH.

AFTER THE BATTLE.

SAUL, ABNER, MICHAL. Chorus of men. All the men excepting DAVID have spears. Women with tabrets enter singing.

No. 1. CHORUS of Women's voices. A Thousand Men.

A thou-sand men Saul left up-on the plain, A thou-sand ten hath Da-vid slain,   A thousand men Saul left up-on the plain, A thou-sand ten hath Da-vid slain,   A

40

No. 2. RECITATIVES.

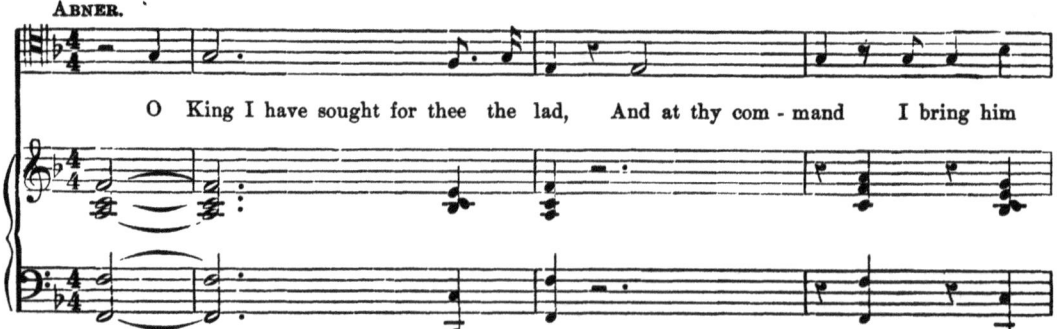

41

SAUL.

hith-er, Me-thinks I have seen that face so fair and rud-dy be-fore; I called a minstrel once to soothe me in my hours of gloom, and this is like him, But the vict-or is worth-y of his crown; whose son art thou?

DAVID.
I am the son of Jes-se the Eph-ra-tite.

SAUL.
The son of the elder of Beth-le-hem. And

42

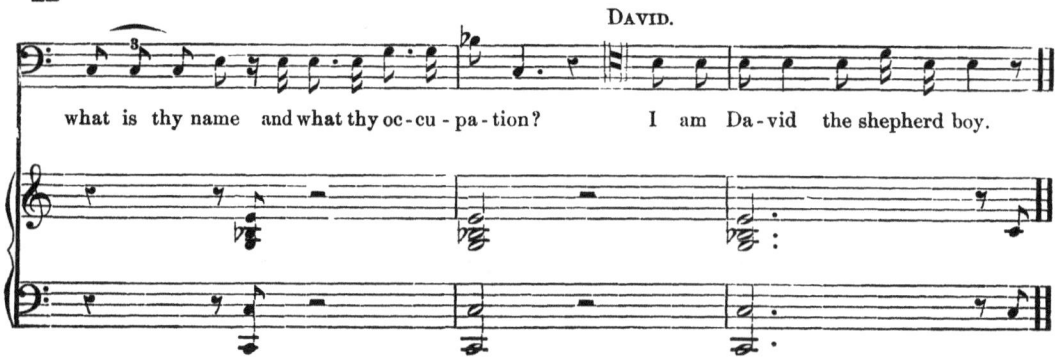

what is thy name and what thy oc-cu-pa-tion? I am Da-vid the shepherd boy.

No. 3. CHORUS continued. A thousand men.

Now take the tabrets and advance, The he-ro hail with song and dance, The he-ro hail with song, with song and dance. Now take the tabrets and advance, The

A thousand men Saul left up-on the plain, A

46

No. 5. SONG. O Lord, Our Lord!

No. 6. CHORUS. When Heroes return.

47

49

51

—SCENE SIXTH.—

DAVID IN EXILE.

DAVID and THREE MEN OF WAR.

No. 1. SONG. In Awful Caverns.

In aw-ful cav-erns wild and dark I hide from man's fierce wrath; Phil - is-tia's lords, with Saul com-bine To hunt my se - cret path; As for the wa-ter pants the hart, Its

52

No. 2. TRIO. But That, Alas!

The men depart.

DAVID *speaks*:
  I do remember well *that* day,
'Twas at the new moon of the plenteous **year**,
I was near Bethlehem's well, beside the **gate**,
When, lo! there came a messenger to me,
And I was called to join my father's family.
I lifted up my face to God, then left

The white sheep in the valleys. An aged
And mysterious man before the altar stood,
Hailed me with gladness, bowed his head, and said:
"The Lord hath chosen *him*." Then he poured
Upon my head the holy oil, and then
He sacrificed a heifer white, then turned away,—
Away, mysteriously, as he had come.

The THREE MEN return as if in haste. The Leader advances to DAVID with a pitcher of water and sings—at first as if somewhat breathless.

No. 3. We Have Broken Our Way.

DAVID *speaks*:
    The Lord forbid:
It is the price of blood. I thirst for it
As thirsts the wounded hart for distant streams,

But it hath cost thee jeopardy. I thirst for God,
And I will pour it out like sacred wine
Upon this bed of flowers, an offering
Unto Him.   (*Pours out the water.*)

No. 4. TRIO. Oh, Why is Thy Soul?

THE THREE MEN OF WAR.

No. 5. SONG. "As pants the hart," and accompanying TRIO, "Why is thy Soul."

hart at eve, For its re-mem - bered streams a -
why do thy foes dis - qui - et bring? Hope thou in God, He hears thy prayer, And thou a - gain his
why do thy foes dis - qui - et bring? Hope thou in God, He hears thy prayer, And thou a - gain his
far, So for . . . . . the Lord my sighs I breathe, So
praise shalt sing, Oh why is thy soul cast down with care? And why do thy foes dis-qui - et bring? Hope
praise shalt sing, Oh why is thy soul cast down with care? And why do thy foes dis-qui - et bring? Hope

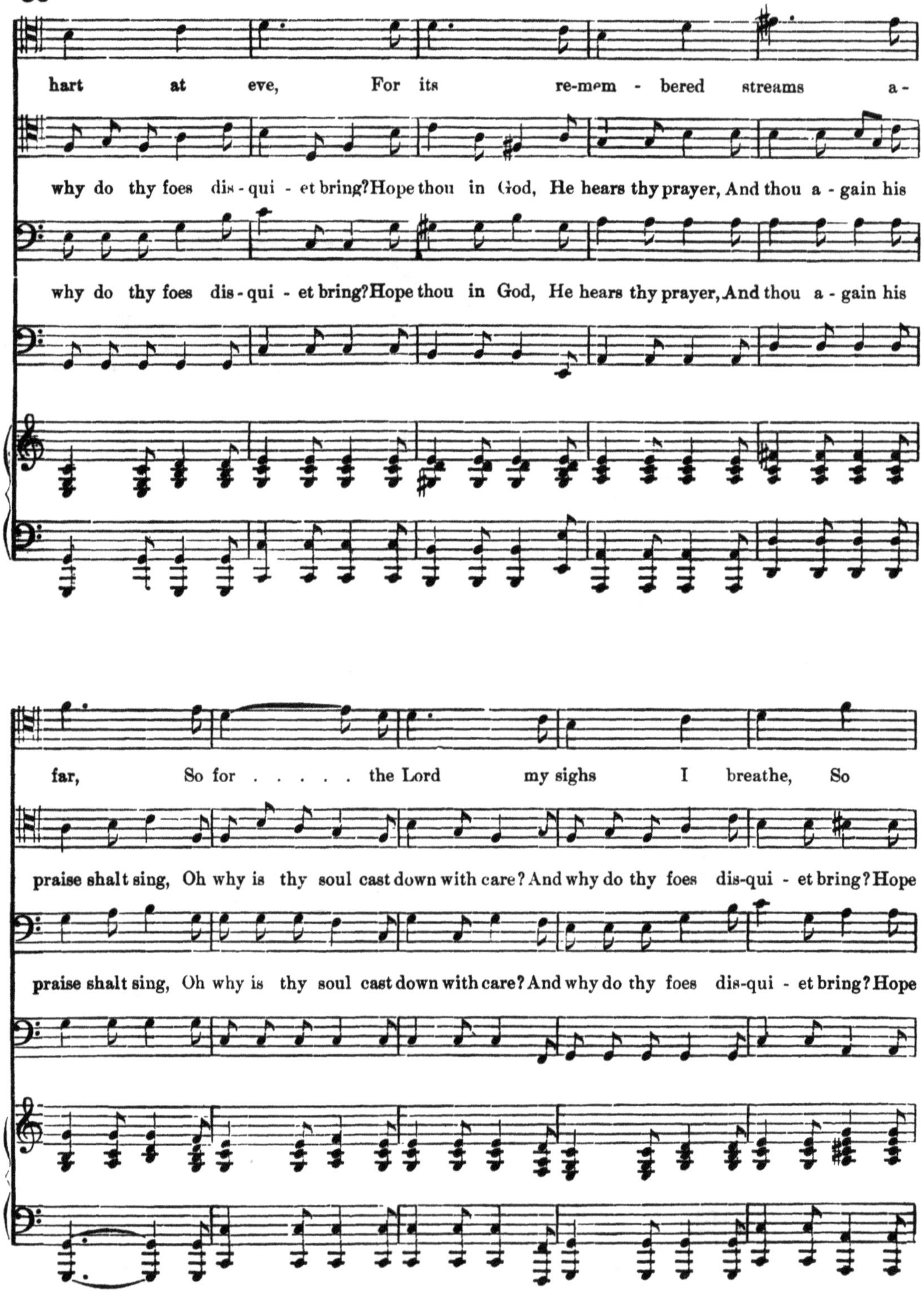

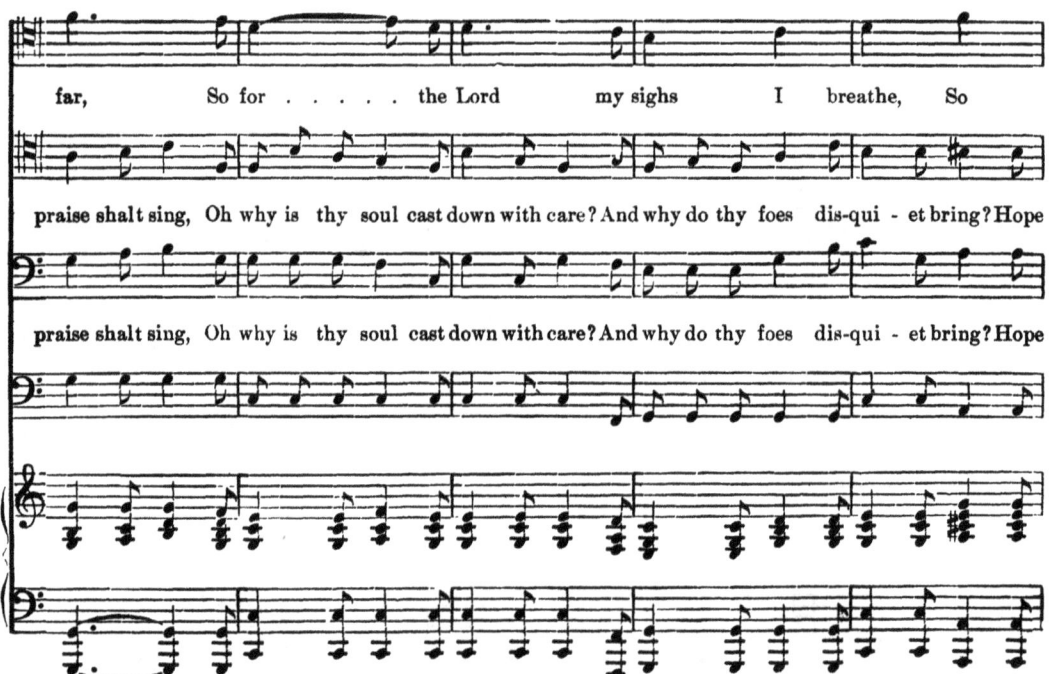

57

CURTAIN FALLS.

for his grace my long - - - - - - - ings are.

thou in God, He hears thy prayer, And thou again his praise, his praise shall sing.

thou in God, He hears thy prayer, And thou again his praise, his praise shall sing.

—SCENE SEVENTH.—

DAVID AND THE SHEPHERD QUEEN.

DAVID, ABIGAIL AND ATTENDANTS, AND SHEPHERDS.

Na-bal doth scorn my suit, Seeks my de-struc-tion, I am a man of

58

No. 2. SCENA. Abigail and Chorus. Peace.

(In all the singing be careful to be well turned toward the audience, and as near it as may be.) (It would be well to omit the 2d verse when the whole Cantata is given.)

62

No. 3. RECITATIVE. Blessed be the Lord, and Peace, concluded.

No. 4. RECITATIVES.

65

CURTAIN FALLS.

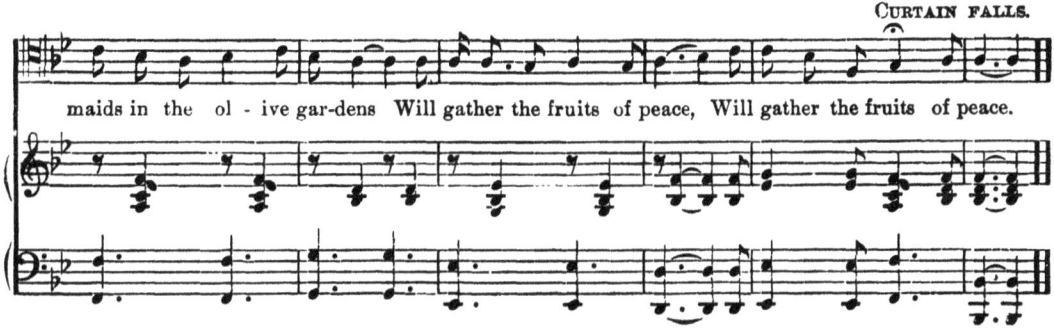

maids in the ol-ive gar-dens Will gather the fruits of peace, Will gather the fruits of peace.

If the children are in front of the platform, they may sing this number before the curtain rises. Otherwise, it may commence after the curtain rises for Scene Eight.

No. 1. The rosy heights of Carmel.

CHILDREN.

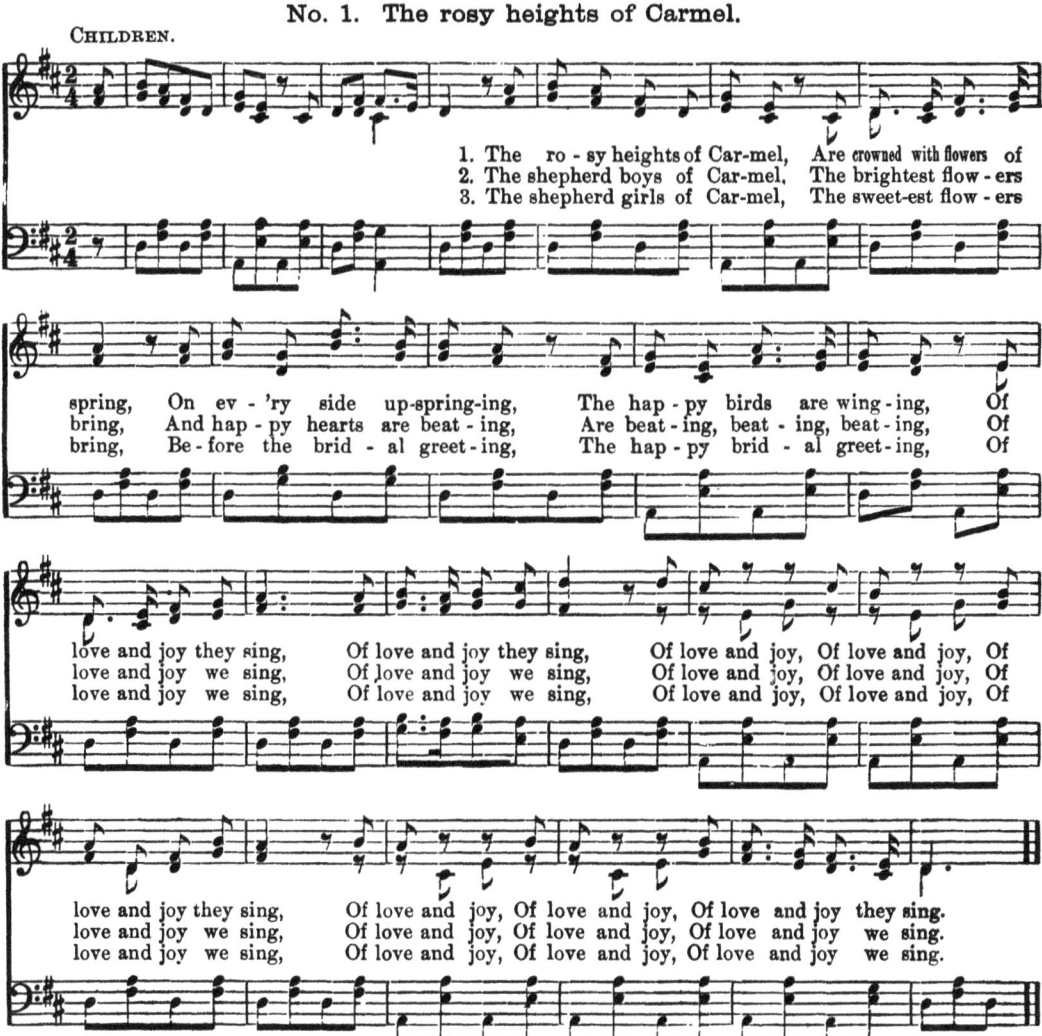

1. The ro-sy heights of Car-mel, Are crowned with flowers of spring, On ev-'ry side up-spring-ing, The hap-py birds are wing-ing, Of love and joy they sing, Of love and joy they sing, Of love and joy, Of love and joy, Of love and joy they sing, Of love and joy, Of love and joy, Of love and joy they sing.

2. The shepherd boys of Car-mel, The brightest flow-ers bring, And hap-py hearts are beat-ing, Are beat-ing, beat-ing, beat-ing, Of love and joy we sing, Of love and joy we sing, Of love and joy, Of love and joy, Of love and joy we sing, Of love and joy, Of love and joy, Of love and joy we sing.

3. The shepherd girls of Car-mel, The sweet-est flow-ers bring, Be-fore the brid-al greet-ing, The hap-py brid-al greet-ing, Of love and joy we sing, Of love and joy we sing, Of love and joy, Of love and joy, Of love and joy we sing, Of love and joy, Of love and joy, Of love and joy we sing.

—SCENE EIGHTH.—

THE CARMELITE BRIDE.

The singers enter, as the instrumental march commences, (some children may be first, if there is room on the platform for them,) with flowers, which they swing to and fro as if throwing them. A little march may be planned—one that will last until the singing commences, or after, if there is room to march and sing. DAVID enters as the *singing* commences.

No. 2. BRIDAL MARCH. From Carmel We Come.

Moderato.

68

ABIGAIL enters with her two attendants. A girl meets her, bearing upon a cushion a wreath which may answer for a crown,—or it may be a crown; The attendants receive it and place it upon ABIGAIL's head.

Then hail her! Then hail her! Then hail her our queen, and her glad praises sing! Yes, hail her and bless her, the bride of our king! From Car - mel we come, with its rich treasures la - den, The bright flow-ers strew, ev - 'ry

70

No. 3. SONG and REFRAIN. Oh, long hast thou wandered.

—SCENE NINTH.—

THE EVENING BEFORE THE CORONATION.

The lights to represent twilight. DAVID **alone.**

DAVID *speaks:*—

    How are the mighty fallen!
Saul, the king of Israel, and Jonathan
Whose love to me was wonderful! On Gilboa
They slumber as they fell together there—
The brave.

    To-morrow is my Coronation day:
The tribes are gathered here to make me king.

    God's ways are wonderful.
Out of the nations of the earth, He Israel chose;
And out of Israel's tribes He Judah chose;
And out of Judah's tribe he chose
My father's family; and out of Jesse's sons,
He chooseth me.

    Goliath fell, and I became
A champion of Israel. When Nabal died
I to my heart received his shepherd queen.
Now Saul and Jonathan are dead, and I become
The king of Israel.

    The night is still.
The oak of Mamre like a giant stands
In the pale moon, and luscious airs are borne
From vine-clad hills, and olive trees and groves
Of shadowy palm. An inspiration in me wakes.
Oh, let me take my harp again, and as
Of old will I awake its chords.

No. 1. HARP SONG. The Lord my Shepherd is.

With harp or imitation of harp, making motions as if playing, while singing his song,

75

fraid. . . . . 3. For

Thou be-fore me still . . . Thy rod and staff shalt bear; Where

en - e-mies en-com-pass me, Thou mak-est my ta - ble

there. . . . . 4. My

No. 2. CHORAL. Evening Hymn.

This hymn is supposed to be sung by the multitude who have gathered for the coronation, and are encamped near by, but out of sight. DAVID alone is on the platform. After each verse the last line of music is repeated with mouths closed—humming, and dying away. A harp accompaniment is written to accompany the humming, but unless the harp pedal of the piano is *very soft*, and the notes can be touched *very delicately*, it is better not to use it. If used, DAVID must appear to accompany.

1. Now star-light soft o'er Car-mel falls, Be-neath the palms we kneel to pray; And faint-ly, 'mid the mountain walls, The murm'-rous voic-es fade a-way.
2. Fa-ther, where'er our tents may be, Where'er our dai-ly con-flicts cease, Thou art our safe-ty still, and we Wilt lay us down and sleep in peace.

Only for the humming interlude. CURTAIN FALLS.

Repeat this strain after each verse, mouths closed.

—SCENE TENTH.—

THE CORONATION.

No. 1. DOUBLE CHORUS. "Hail," and "Manasseh sends her Thousands."

This brings in all the singers excepting MICHAL, SAMUEL and SAUL. Those voices may aid if costumes are changed, as they are out of sight. An elevation to answer as a throne in center. DAVID in front of it; ABIGAIL by his side. The ELDER who is to crown DAVID, and sing the bass in the quartett, near, as are also ABIGAIL's attendants, who are to sing Soprano and Alto in quartett.

DAVID comes forward and kneels or bows while the crown is placed upon his head by the ELDER. He then rises and takes his place on the elevation. The quartet join him and they commence the following number in exact time at the close of this interlude.

No. 2. INTERLUDE during the crowning.

May be repeated if not long enough.

84

85

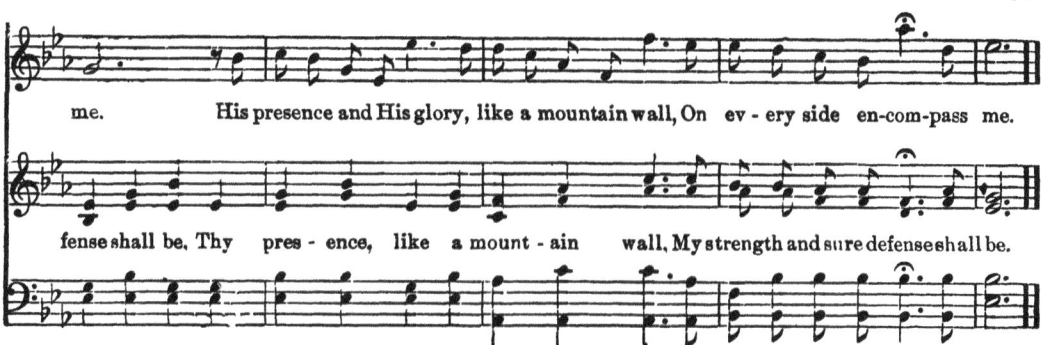

No. 4. FINALE. "Hosanna! Blessed is He that Cometh." (with Obligato for Soprano and Tenor.)

86

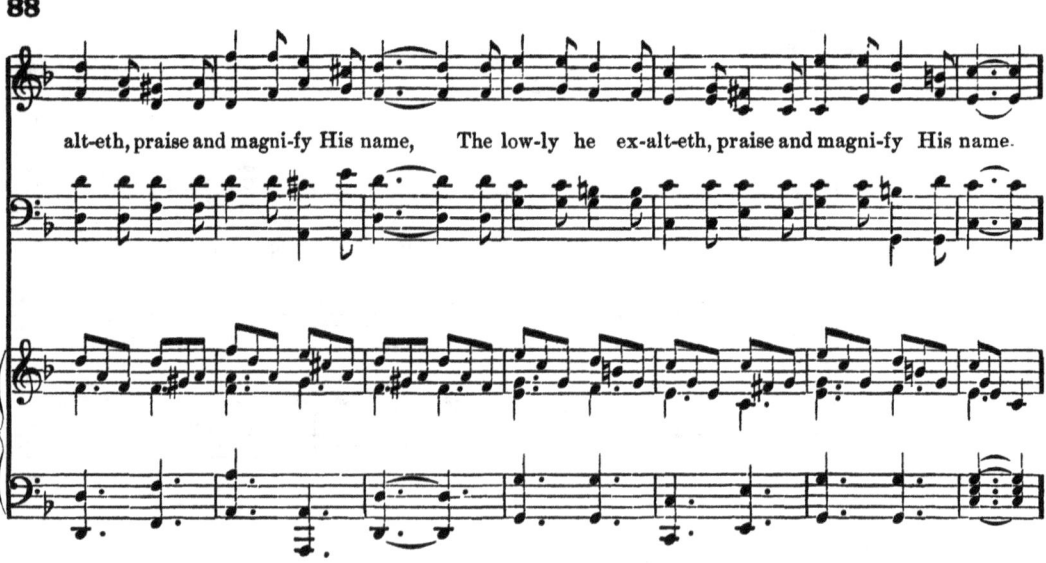

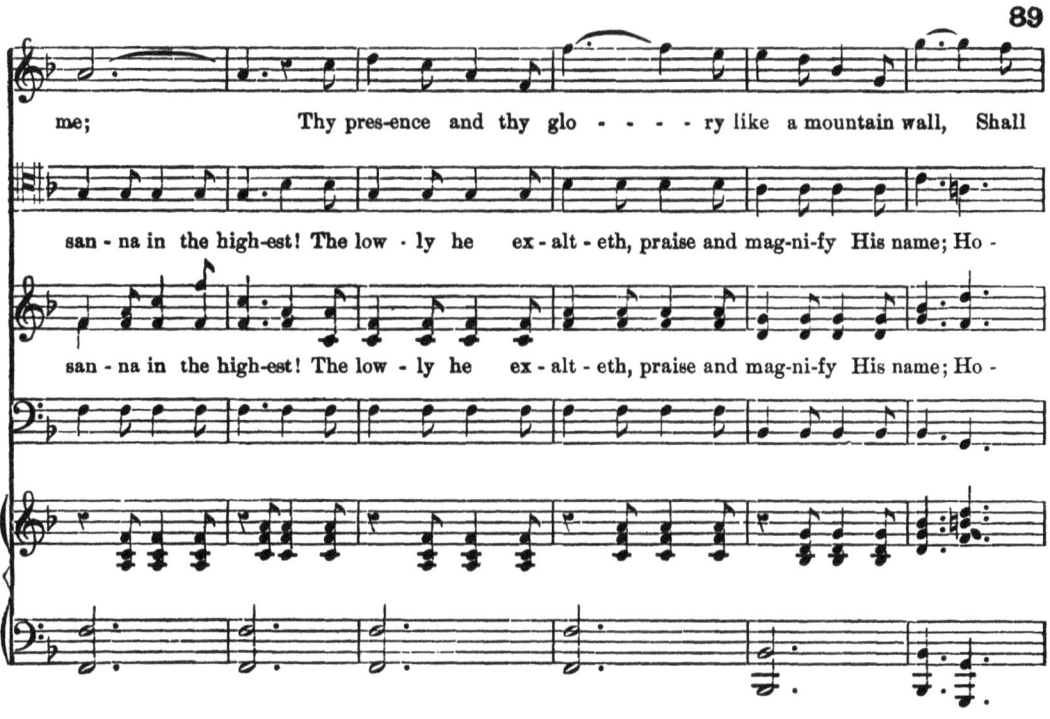

www.ingramcontent.com/pod-product-compliance
Lightning Source LLC
Chambersburg PA
CBHW080522110426
42742CB00017B/3208